AS EASY

Memorize the Morse code using fun Illustrations

- Sanyukta Bhatnagar

To the most important people in my life...

My sweet daughter Miraya, for whom I started illustrating this...

And to my awesome partner Shikhar, without whom I would've taken years to finish this ;)

WHY MORSE ?

Have you tried writing coded letters to your friends in school or do you write your personal diary in coded words to keep it secret?
Almost everyone loves to be a Spy. And everyone has the potential to be one.
All you need is keen eyes, open ears and a secret language. So you can pass on the secret information without somebody's notice!
One of such code is "Morse".

I am sure, you must've heard of it.

Made by an American Artist Samuel Morse in 1844, it really was a popular means of communication during the World Wars. Hundreds of Spies used it on daily basis to exchange information and save the world!
Though now we are not at war, It's still fun and very useful to know it.

Morse can come in handy at teamwork, play and even at distress situations. It can be transmitted in lots of ways.
Originally used as electrical pulses along a telegraph wire, it can also be used as an audio tone, a radio signal with short and long tones, or as a mechanical, audible or visual signal like toggling a common flashlight, keying a radio on and off, flashing a mirror or even a car horn.

Some mine rescuers used rope by pulling it with short pull for a dot and a long pull for a dash.

An important use of Morse code is signaling for help through SOS, "· · · — — — · · ·".
SOS is not three separate characters, it is a pro-sign SOS and is keyed without gaps between characters.

There are many other creative ways to practice this code. Like using flash lights or tapping or even blinking eyes.
But have you ever find it difficult to remember all the dots and dashes, which represent the alphabets?

Well, here is a fun way to learn and memorize the Morse Alphabets.
I am hopeful, this book will serve you good in all of your adventures.
Who knows, it may be your first step to become (Hush!!) ... A Secret Spy!

- Sanyukta

READERS GUIDE FOR MORSE

B

■ ● ● ●

DAH DIT DIT DIT

C

DAH DIT DAH DIT

D

DAH DIT DIT

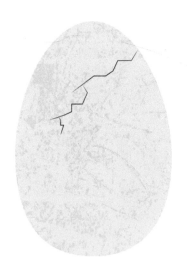

DIT

F

● ● ▬ ●

DIT DIT DAH DIT

G

DAH DAH DIT

H

• • • •

DIT DIT DIT DIT

I

DIT DIT

J

● ▬ ▬ ▬

DIT DAH DAH DAH

DAH DIT DAH

L

DIT DAH DIT DIT

DAH DAH

O

▬ ▬ ▬

DAH DAH DAH

P

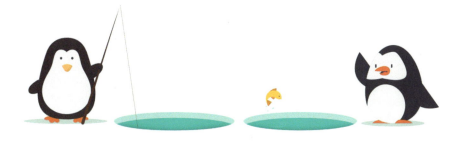

DIT DAH DAH DIT

Q

DAH DAH DIT DAH

R

● ▬ ●

DIT DAH DIT

S

● ● ●
DIT DIT DIT

T

DAH

DIT DIT DAH

● ▬ ▬

DIT DAH DAH

DAH DIT DIT DAH

Y

DAH DIT DAH DAH

DAH DAH DIT DIT

1

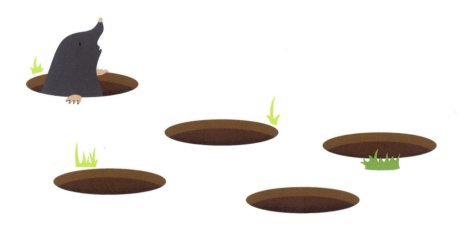

DIT DAH DAH DAH DAH

2

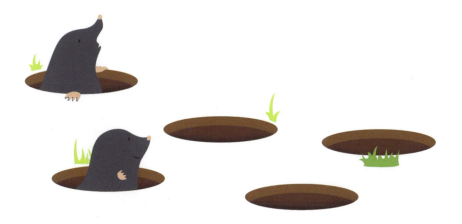

DIT DIT DAH DAH DAH

3

DIT DIT DIT DAH DAH

● ● ● ● ▬

DIT DIT DIT DIT DAH

5

● ● ● ● ●

DIT DIT DIT DIT DIT

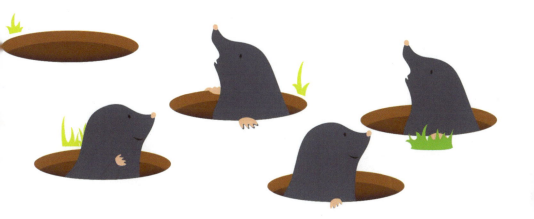

■ ● ● ● ●

DAH DIT DIT DIT DIT

7

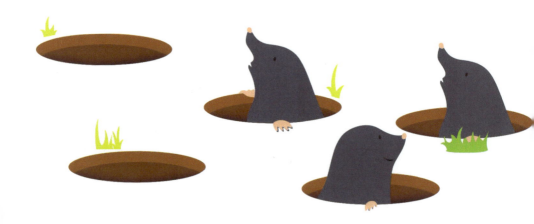

DAH DAH DIT DIT DIT

8

DAH DAH DAH DIT DIT

q

DAH DAH DAH DAH DIT

READERS GUIDE FOR MORSE

REPRESENTATION AND SPACES

Short mark or "Dit" is one time unit long.

longer mark or "dah" is three time units long.

Gap between the dots and dashes in a character is one dot duration or one unit long.

Gap between words is seven time units long.

End of the word is represented by "/" (when typed)

TRANSMISSION

Morse code can be transmitted in lots of ways.

Originally used as electrical pulses along a telegraph wire, it can also be used as an audio tone, a radio signal with short and long tones, or as a mechanical, audible or visual signal like toggling a common flashlight, keying a radio on and off, flashing a mirror or even a car horn.

Some mine rescues used rope by pulling it with short pull for a dot and a long pull for a dash.

An important use of Morse code is signalling for help through SOS, "· · · — — — · · ·".

SOS is not three separate characters, it is a prosign SOS and is keyed without gaps between characters.

CPSIA information can be obtained
at www.ICGtesting.com
Printed in the USA
LVHW07n0059200818
587482LV00001B/7/P